Easy To Break, Hard To Build

How To Effectively Build

Trust With Others

I0454550

Destiny S. Harris

...

. . .

Copyright

Copyright © 2023 Destiny S. Harris.

I don't care if you share my work. Just be sure to create work of your own. You have infinite creative ability; use it.

Front cover image by Destiny S. Harris.
Book design by Destiny S. Harris.
First printing edition 2023.
www.destinyh.com

...

. . .

Dedication

This book is dedicated to you

...

. . .

A Gift For You

Thank you for taking the time to read this book. As a token of my appreciation, here is a gift to you.

I give away free books daily. Here's how to get your free books today:

Step 1: Visit amazon.com/author/destinyharris

Step 2: Filter books by "Price: Low to High"

Step 3: Download available free books

. . .

. . .

Table of Contents

. . .

. . .

...

Introduction

The focus of this book was originally on handling disappointment, but then the book ended up writing itself with a focus on building trust with others.

Moving in a completely different direction, trust is a worthy subject to review.

You can only build trust with others by first getting your act together.

To be an effective leader, communicator, and relationship builder, you must learn to cultivate trusting relationships with others.

Quality relationships start with us.

Quality communication starts with us.

If you're disappointed with your results in your professional and personal relationships, there is one common denominator: **you**.

This book is relatively short but provides valuable tools to help you uplevel your relationships.

The areas we will review in this book include the following:

1. Manage Others' Expectations of You

2. Keep Your Word

3. Encourage Others' Relentlessly

4. Go Out Of Your Way For Others

5. Love People Even If They Let You Down And Take The Fall

6. An Effective Leader And Communicator

7. Study

. . .

. . .

Chapter 1: Manage Others' Expectations of You

Phil (Bill's Boss): Hey Bill, do you still have the capacity to take on two additional direct reports on top of managing the two teams you have now?

Bill: Absolutely. That's no problem at all.

Meanwhile, Bill is underwater and falling behind even though he started his new job less than 30 days ago.

This is a perfect example of setting oneself up for failure by unsuccessfully delivering valuable results.

In this case, Bill ended up being let go. Not because he wasn't a good employee but because he couldn't communicate effectively and manage expectations.

We can't prevent ourselves from disappointing others, but we can mitigate disappointment by not overcommitting and being transparent.

When we practice this, we also teach others to relinquish their egos and do the same.

If you already have taken on plenty of responsibility, just say **no**; it's one of the most powerful words. Yet, many use it too infrequently.

Everyone wants to be a superhero, but being a superhero on top of our daily obligations is not always realistic.

When we keep our promises to ourselves, we also increase our confidence.

When we hold ourselves accountable to ourselves, we increase our confidence.

Our reputation with ourselves is more crucial than our reputation with others.

The most important person you keep your word to is <u>yourself</u>.

...

...

Chapter 2: Keep Your Word

Sal: I will get that brief over to you by midnight tomorrow.

Midnight tomorrow comes and goes, and Larry wonders where the brief is.

As mentioned in the previous chapter, sometimes, we set ambitious expectations for ourselves and others.

If you believe you can't make a deadline, don't set one **or** give yourself plenty of buffer time to allow enough leeway for you to deliver on your promise.

The worst thing you can do for your reputation is underdeliver.

In the past, I have undelivered because I had an underlying problem: overcommitment.

The best strategy is to always under-promise and over-deliver or, at minimum, promise and deliver.

Every time you underdeliver, you jeopardize your reputation and sever your trust with others.

. . .

...

Chapter 3: Encourage Others Relentlessly

One of my favorite stories is in John C. Maxwell's "25 Ways to Win With People" book.

In the book, he talks about how, during his nephew's baseball game, he pulled his discouraged nephew aside and told him, "Son, all you have to do in the game of baseball is hit the ball. That's it."

His nephew was shocked and questioned if baseball was really *that* simple. John was adamant and instilled belief in this truth.

So, his nephew went back on the field. When the ball came, he missed. And he missed again. And he missed again. But soon, he started hitting the ball.

No matter if his nephew hit the ball or didn't hit the ball, John was encouraging every play.

If his nephew struck out, he would shout, "That's the best strikeout I've ever seen in my life.'

Though others were judging John and his nephew, his nephew was building belief and confidence in himself.

Years later, his nephew was off to college but felt compelled to stop at his Uncle John's house.

He told Uncle John thank you for all the encouragement during his baseball games; it led him to win a baseball scholarship.

All it took was some belief and encouragement.

...

. . .

Chapter 4: Go Out Of Your Way

I enjoy sitting in the aisle seat of the planes. If someone is sitting by me, I usually check to learn what their bag looks like before they sit down with me.

If I don't notice their bag before they sit next to me, I ask what their bag looks like when the plane lands, and then I get it out for them.

I do this out of simple courtesy. People notice when you go out of your way for them. Moreover, it creates a ripple effect.

They might be kinder to someone on their path that day or do the same thing the next time an opportunity presents itself.

Pay attention to people and anticipate their needs. How can you make their lives easier?

Don't seek for anything in return; do it because it feels good and because life is better when you're helping people.

. . .

. . .

Chapter 5: Love People Even When They Let You Down & Take The Fall

I had a deadline that required help from a friend back in the States while I was abroad.

Thankfully, they were up for the task and signed up to help me immediately. I was overcome with gratitude since I was in a bind.

But when it was time to deliver, they were nowhere to be found.

At first, I was disappointed; this person made it a point to overdeliver and overpromise. But I realized it was partly my fault. Maybe I was unclear with my timeline of when I needed the task to be completed.

So, I put myself out there and patiently asked how they were doing. I then apologized for the last-minute request on top of their busy schedule and for potentially miscommunicating the deadline. Finally, I asked if they were still able to deliver.

It was one of the most humbling things I ever did; in the past, it was easy to write people off and assume malice.

One could think thoughts such as:

- They're so unreliable.
- How could they forget about me?
- Rely on yourself and no one else.
- Are they trying to screw me over?
- People never hold their end of the bargain.

I found out that my friend got the task completed the day prior but forgot to submit it because they were in the middle of another project.

Either way, the friend immediately sent over the deliverable and apologized.

I'm not going to act like I wasn't affected by their delayed delivery.

My friend let me down because I was committed to their timeline and had set expectations with others dependent on the timeline.

Sometimes people let you down. Instead of getting angry or frustrated, love them, treat them with respect, exude patience, and thank them for their efforts.

Ultimately, I got what I needed in the nick of time because I set a buffer (always set a buffer on your timelines), which meant I could still deliver within an hour past the deadline.

But it did make me question whether I could rely on them again, which boils down to trust. When you say you're going to deliver, deliver. And always deliver before a deadline.

But you might also be able to take it as an opportunity to improve your communication.

In this situation, I learned that **I** need to be more precise by asking the following questions:

1. I need the deliverable by x date. Does that fit into your schedule?

2. Okay, you said x date works for you. Can I let the team know that this is a good date to expect it from you?

3. Awesome. Do you mind if I check in with you before the deadline to ensure we're aligned, or if you need more time?

Frequently, people miss deadlines because there is a lack of communication, not malicious intent.

Who failed in this situation? Both parties. But a leader always takes the fall.

Though my friend could have communicated better, so could I. I took the blame for this and took it as a lesson to communicate more effectively in all matters going forward.

What If Things Don't Improve?

A conversation is warranted if things don't improve over time after establishing clearer communication.

No matter what result occurs, avoid getting overly emotional.

Focus on communicating your needs directly and respectfully. And be sure you walk the walk you talk.

Never request anything from someone else you're unwilling to give yourself.

. . .

. . .

Chapter 6: An Effective Leader And Communicator

The best leaders and communicators are the ones that focus on people.

They're not self-centered or obsessed with the spotlight.

They're not narcissists or focused only on themselves.

Instead, they constantly seek to learn and explore others.

What are the people around them going through, what are their needs, and how can they help them?

How can they make the people around them feel more love, respect, and value?

This is what an effective leader and a good communicator prioritizes above all else.

If a relationship fails, what is their responsibility for the failure, and how can they make it successful again? It only takes one person to shift a relationship around, and it tends to be the person with higher self-awareness and less ego; make it a point to be this person consistently.

When you implement a more servant leadership style, you will experience more meaningful results from your personal and professional relationships.

Ask yourself how you can implement more servant-style leadership and communication in all of your relationships.

Don't wait to implement change; implement it now.

Start with the closest people to you, which can include your family.

The next time you get irritated or find your family member unreasonable, take a step back and learn how to approach the relationship differently to produce a more productive outcome.

If your partner or spouse's behavior isn't cutting lately, seek the good and focus on it. Praise them for it. In the meantime, improve yourself and your interactions with them.

. . .

...

Chapter 7: Study

My brother told me I needed to work on emotional intelligence. Much of my family historically told me I can be harsh and not as good with people. Instead of taking it personally, I finally took it on as a challenge to become more skilled in managing relationships with people.

I'm still far from perfect, but I'm dedicated to learning, and I now have dedicated mentors I'm learning from who are helping me improve my interactions with people.

Another thing that is elevating me is reading.

Since my brother told me that piece of feedback, I've been reading books on psychology, leadership, emotional intelligence, and communication.

It's taken several books to start noticing a shift, but I'm slowly improving.

. . .

...

Thank You For Reading

Thank you for reading this book.

Stay blessed, lucky, favored, aware, joyous, and committed to bettering yourself.

. . .

. . .

The End.

...

...

About Destiny S. Harris

Destiny S. Harris' goal is to positively inspire, cultivate, elevate, and educate the minds of individuals across the globe through her writing.

Creating (whether books, courses, articles, poetry, or music) has always been Destiny's thing, not to mention health & fitness and all things entrepreneurial. Destiny published her first book, "Beauty Secrets for Girls," at age 11 and her second book, "Don't Wait Until It's Too Late," at age 12.

Destiny obtained three degrees in Psychology, Political Science, & Cultural Studies. She also started her own music teaching business at the age of 14, which she led for over ten years. In addition, she has been teaching academic, career, and personal development topics to thousands of students and readers since 2004.

Outside of writing, Destiny loves and enjoys a few other things: reading, weightlifting, traveling, football, dogs, food, classic movies, mountain and ocean views, sleeping, plants, and nature.

Check out her work, leave a review, share your thoughts with your friends and family, and be a part of a movement: helping people learn and grow through means of self-education (books).

Complete the Steps To Get Free eBooks:

Step 1: Go to amazon.com/author/destinyharris

Step 2: Filter books by "Price: Low to High"

Step 3: Download available free books

. . .

. . .

Connect W/ Destiny S. Harris

Please reach out and stay in touch. Destiny S. Harris enjoys chatting with readers.

Start a conversation today @ destinyh.com

. . .

. . .

Free Gifts!

Access courses & free eBooks at the link below:

destinyh.com

. . .

. . .